HOW TO ESCAPE
THE DIGITAL WORLD

and Enjoy Reality

In Just 45 Minutes a Day!

INSTRUCTIONS:

1. Turn off all your devices

2. Set your clock for 45 minutes.

3. Turn to the next page in this book.

4. Read, Write, Draw, Dream & Color!

5. Use ONE day's worth of pages at a time

to help you unwind and refocus.

6. DON'T Look Ahead!

Created By: Sarah Janisse Brown & Includes Artwork by: Natasha Chetkova

The Thinking Tree Publishing Company, LLC Copyright 2016 – Do Not Copy

STILLSMILING.NET

Day 1

I Am Living in Digital World,

BUT I AM NOT A DIGITAL GIRL!

I am not a digital image.

I may not be a great artist,

but I am going to pick up a pen or pencil

and draw a picture of me,

just enjoying my life, unplugged.

In the real world.

MY FAVORITE PLACE

ON EARTH:

Hopes & Dreams
& Real things

Paper books and clicking clocks

Hiking boots, and warm wool socks.

A backpack stuffed with hopes and dreams.

And a heart longing for real things.

Clouds above and dancing trees,

Whispered prayers and wild seas.

A little boat, and you with me.

Can't this be our reality?

Firewood and ocean waves,

Determination, strong and brave.

No clicks, no likes, no shares, no saves.

Just you and me, finding our way.

If we leave behind a thousand friends,

Perhaps we'll find each other.

We'll learn how to begin again,

By living real life together.

"I think that the more and more we focus on media the more distance we put between us and our loved ones and the natural world. I think that the longer we do this the thicker our screen becomes and we will have a harder time actually seeing what we are missing!"

Shalie Gilson

REAL FRIENDS.

We care about each other.

1.

2.

3.

4.

5.

6.

My friends are not digital images.

They are real people,

with real lives, and real needs.

Most of all,

my friends need...

My Friends Need...

Draw or Write about one fun thing

To do before you get back online!

The joy of living Life outside of a screen is noticing all the beauty that surrounds you. Though technology is the easiest way to communicate with family and friends, it will never replace the warmth of a family dinner, a cup of tea with a friend, a giggle with your teenager. All we have to do is look up.

Dawn Kilgore

How can I love
each unique friend in a
NON-DIGITAL WAY?

1.

2.

3.

4.

5.

6.

Friends are not just faces on phones and iPads and laptops. They are real human beings with eyes, ears, hearts, feelings, fears and needs.

REAL LIFE IDEAS
FOR HAVING FUN TOGETHER!

I Want To Be More Like...

_____

_____

_____

_____

_____

_____

Draw or Write about one fun thing

To do before you get back online!

" A quick trip outside, usually to my favorite park, is my go-to plan for getting back in touch with reality... and nature... and especially God. We truly must unplug in order to recharge. Naturally! "

Robin Resch

MAKE A HAPPY
TO-DO-LIST

There are many things

I want to do in real life.

What little things

could I do each day,

to make the world around me

A better place?

Make a List of 8 little things,

that take 8 minutes or less,

That can bring joy

into my real life...

SIX LITTLE THINGS TO MAKE MY WORLD HAPPIER!

I Am Grateful for...

_____

_____

_____

_____

_____

_____

Draw or Write about one fun thing

To do before you get back online!

"Technology is an amazing tool for gathering information and connecting with people, but there is a time and place for that and it shouldn't be all the time. I don't want to miss out on seeing my own children and connecting with them when I have the chance. "

"It isn't just technology that distracts us. Consciously being aware that we need to connect with the people around us is crucial. "

"Homeschooling means I am with my kids all the time and I can forget that even though we are always together they still need me to stop and look them in the eye and speak to them and see who they are. "

Lynne' Sleiman

NEWS FEED

You became my news today.

It was bad news.

But I "liked" it anyway.

Thirty-six "friends" agreed to pray.

But no one had a lot to say.

Scroll down, a moment later.

Your heartbreak is your own.

I'm watching cats and dogs dance across my screen.

Dancing and setting me free from your reality.

In real life this would never be.

I would have been there holding you,

Crying too. By your side.

But all I have to do today is "like"

And you know you had my click, just for a moment.

Now, I'm ashamed to be laughing

At the cats and dogs dancing,

when I should have stopped the world

to really love you, my friend.

REAL WAYS TO HELP A FRIEND IN NEED:

I Want To ...

_____

_____

_____

_____

_____

_____

_____

Draw or Write about one fun thing

To do before you get back online!

"My sweet aunt has been diagnosed with brain cancer and only given 2 to 4 months to live and it's really opened my eyes. Facebook is fun and I use it to keep up with out of town family but my eyes have been opened to what's important. Family & friends. Playing with my kids. Loving on my hubby. Hanging out with friends. Grilling out. Serving others. That's important... not the virtual world! "

Amy Whitaker

LOST SISTER

Where have you been today?

Did your phone break?

Did the Mom or Dad take your Wi-Fi Away?

Maybe you forgot to pay.

Does it matter anyway?

Should I wonder if something is wrong?

I'll just watch a video and listen to another song.

I messaged you, but no reply.

Six more hours have gone by.

I ask the world and click "send".

Everyone is online, but you, my friend.

Eight hours have now gone past.

Where was it that I saw you last?

On Facebook?

On Skype?

On Twitter?

I better get up, get off my bed,

go down the hall, to your room instead,

and check on you, my sister.

THINGS TO DO AT HOME WITH MY FAMILY:

I Will Never Forget When...

I went to go get my
dog j.p.

Draw or Write about one fun thing

To do before you get back online!

"When reality meets virtual reality, discontentment starts. Purpose to push forward, unplug and notice the mundane. For in the mundane of life lies the holy—the precious—the very purpose of life. "

Jennifer Church Newsom

PAPER BOOKS

I opened up a book today.

I felt the softness of each page.

I could smell the paper,

warming in the sunlight.

It was beautiful, quiet, and strange.

One word flowed after another.

Everything was black and white.

So clear to me.

Each page set ablaze

a mystery, full of color, in my mind.

I knew I wasn't wasting time.

So I turned another page.

I didn't click, I didn't share, I didn't like.

There were no advertisements on the right.

With each new chapter my heart found it's delight

As a quiet day became a peaceful night.

Think of six things to read about in paper books:

I Need to Change the Way...

_____

_____

_____

_____

_____

_____

_____

Draw or Write about one fun thing

To do before you get back online!

OUTSIDE

Why do you stay inside?

The sun is shining.

Why hide behind a screen?

When you could be free.

Have you forgotten how to breath?

Little bird, you were not made

to stay trapped Inside a cage.

Looking but not experiencing

All the wonders of the world.

The real world waits outside...

And it's warm

It's cold.

It's soft,

It's sweet,

It's bright,

It's wild,

It's amazing.

It's a lot like you.

Unplug. Untangle. Unwind.

Leave your device behind.

Explore your world.

SIX INTERESTING THINGS
TO DO OUTSIDE

I Need to Go...

_____

_____

_____

_____

_____

_____

_____

Draw or Write about one fun thing

To do before you get back online!

"There was a big period where I wanted so much to be the perfect parent and homeschooler that I spent hours on the Internet to learn and be inspired. One day I realized I was so busy trying to learn how to live this perfect life that I was failing to truly live it. All the hours I'd been spending trying to inspire and motive myself when I could have just gotten up and done something."

Caroline McConnell

Funny

Caroline McConnall

Funny how we can know someone's face,

How they look,

the words they say,

and the image they broadcast to the world,

But we don't really know them.

We see the polished side,

The edited side,

The "I don't want anyone to see any bad

things about me" side.

We often hear their statuses,

broadcasted like newspaper articles,

We read them,

we like them,

and respond to them.

This little world,

has become our lives.

We involve ourselves deeply,

in the lives of others on our 'lists'.

But become so preoccupied,

we don't look each other in the face.

We feel so involved,

but we hardly lift a physical finger.

We feel as though we have so many

friends,

but find ourselves alone,

And when alone,

we have no clue who to call.

Scanning the pages of 'friends',

we feel this odd feeling,

as we realize,

there isn't a connection.

One after another,

the faces blur.

Their statuses blur,

and we wonder,

Do we know them at all?

Have we seen them?

Talked physically to them?

Been involved in anyway?

OR do we feel online is enough?

It checks something off our list?

The emptiness,

We feel it, don't we?

As we sit around with those we know,

but we don't know them.

We can't talk to them,

or reach out to them,

because we are all so distant,

lost in our own worlds,

the worlds where we pride ourselves,

knowing each others faces...

And even as I write this,

I find it all to be true,

You think you know me...

but do I even really know you?

KNOW THE REAL ME

Overlook my little flaws.

Overlook my small mistakes.

What you see, the real me, I also saw,

And was afraid to be, just me.

Do you know where I've been?

How far I've come, Or what it takes,

To let you in, and see the real me?

So overlook the silly things

that make no sense to you.

I'm just living out the truth, in front of you.

I'm not photo-shopping me.

What I am is what you see.

No pretending, no hiding behind screens.

Sometimes I'll say what I don't mean.

There's no "cut, or paste" and no delete.

So I'll mess up, and so will you,

But let's learn to forgive.

We will live and learn and laugh outload

And I'll hear you and you'll see me.

Face to face, as it was meant to be.

And I'll be, the real me.

WHAT MY REAL FRIENDS KNOW ABOUT ME:

I Need to Say...

_____

_____

_____

_____

_____

_____

_____

Draw or Write about one fun thing

To do before you get back online!

1734 FRIENDS

She thinks she has 1734 Friends.

She posts, and shares and likes a lot of things.

Her profile picture looks just like a girl

On the cover of seventeen, a magazine.

In her selfies she always smiles.

Yes, she laughs, she flirts, she promises

that everything is always going to turn out fine.

She's a "friend" of yours and she's a "friend" of mine.

She doesn't feel as pretty as her picture.

She only shares the good news, not the bad.

She's all alone, afraid, and she's like a little child

So she plays hide and seek behind a false identity.

What she really needs is just a few good friends.

What she really needs is honestly and truth.

What she really needs is hope, and faith and Jesus.

What she really needs is real friend in you.

WHAT CAN I DO TO HELP OTHERS EMBRACE REALITY?

"Don't compare your insides with someone else's outsides."

R. N. Lawson

I Will Spend More of My Time...

_____

_____

_____

_____

_____

_____

_____

Draw or Write about one fun thing
To do before you get back online!

TAKE A WALK

Come take a walk with me

Come sit beneath a tree,

Come talk with me face to face.

Come have a cup of tea,

Don't be a mystery,

Leave all your gadgets behind.

Don't take another call,

You'll miss the colors of Fall

You'll miss the new life of Spring

Come now and walk with me,

There's so much more to see

Feel the cool wind and warm sun

Can you see down the road?

Look where the river flows

Hold my hand as we run.

WHAT DO YOU LOVE MOST ABOUT THE SEASONS?

If I Had a Second Chance...

_____

_____

_____

_____

_____

_____

_____

Draw or Write about one fun thing

To do before you get back online!

How Much Screen Time
do I Need Each Day?

How Much Time Should do I Need
With God Each Day?

How Much Time Should I Spend with
Family and with my Friends?

I Am Becoming...

_____

_____

_____

_____

_____

_____

Draw or Write about one fun thing

To do before you get back online!

HERE I AM, FEARLESS

Here I am waiting, the world is quiet.

Here I am trusting, the sun has set.

Here I am living, though storms are stirring.

Here I am chasing a dream.

I've left the safely of my four walls.

I've walked out the doors with no phone.

I'm quite certain that I am still safe

Although I feel so alone.

I watch the storm clouds gather.

I watch the stars disappear.

I hear the rumble of thunder

As lighting flashes,, I face my fear

I feel so brave and courageous

In the face of the storm as it blows

I feel so free, like the wind that I breathe

Let the rain come soak my clothes!

WHAT FEARS DO
I NEED TO FACE?

My Next Adventure Will Be...

become a
My Goals:
vet

Amandas vet

Help all animals
My Plans:

Be succsessful
My Hopes:

"We don't need to throw technology out the window, we just need to use it well and put it in its place. In 20 years I won't look back at my life and wish I hadn't missed out on that social media news tidbit, but I will likely look back and wish I had watched my children more closely and cherished them and listened to them when I had the chance."

Lynne' Sleiman

ENJOY REALITY

Use A Page or Two

As a Reward,

Whenever You

Log Off

UnPlug

And need to Unwind!

And then go do Something!

Draw

Dream

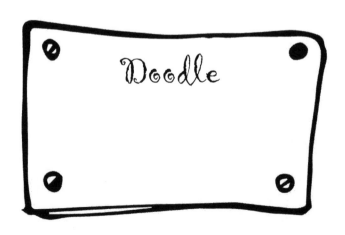

Doodle

New Beginnings...

I love being able to really be in tune with my
kids and what is going on in their lives. When
I am away from social media it allows me
more time to invest in the lives of my husband
and kids and those I come in contact with.

Martina Chymist Bump

"I work on Facebook, networking and marketing my business. However, my primary "business" is what is happening in the hearts and minds of my children. The screens in my life can never replace or overshadow their smiles or I will be out of balance."

Heather Randall

"I feel like I am constantly vacillating between struggling against technology and succumbing to it. It is impossible to escape the technology, I need to find better balance with it. "

Candice Forte

"No one posts the bad pictures... As I scroll through my friends' pictures I see beauty, strength, and grace. If I look around me I can see those same things... maybe even in the mirror."

Randi Banning

HOPES, DREAMS & PRAYERS...

Connect with your family! Talk to them, play with them, talk to your husband, talk to God! There are lots of people out there whom we have not called and told them how much we and God loves them.

Perez

Do something fun with the family, an art project, a field trip, gardening, bike, etc. And if the house is falling apart, we can teach out kids to help us with chores in a fun and productive way, if we all help then the work is done faster and we have more free time for each other and maybe even to read a book alone for a little bit.

Perez

I should turn the computer off and actually connect with my kids. Being present doesn't mean being in the same room as them. It means to meet them where they are at, to know their heart, their joys & fears, to fill their love tanks and make precious memories. I don't want to miss any more time with my amazing family.

Michelle Bradford

I need to be focusing on the soul of my child instead of the souls of Facebook. To ponder and cherish the children God has given me as a vocation instead of comparing and stealing joy from the beautiful life in front of me. I need to be present and taste and see the life in my house right now.

Christy Thomas

HOPES, DREAMS & PRAYERS...

Right now, I should be **living**! I'm guilty of spending too much time on social media, staring at a screen is not living! I should be praying, and thanking God for all my blessings. I should be teaching and guiding my children through the little struggles of life. I should be **outside** breathing the fresh air and connecting with nature. We are all only given a limited number of minutes to be alive... How many will you spend **living**?

Jenn Poulin

HOPES, DREAMS & PRAYERS...

HOPES, DREAMS & PRAYERS...

32332529R00058

Made in the USA
San Bernardino, CA
03 April 2016